Essentials of Work Study

(Method Study and Work Measurement)

Shyam Bhatawdekar
Dr Kalpana Bhatawdekar

Essentials of Work Study
(Method Study and Work Measurement)

Books by Shyam Bhatawdekar and Dr Kalpana Bhatawdekar

Management, Business, Self-help and Personality Development Books

1. HSoftware (Human Software) (The Only Key to Higher Effectiveness) https://www.amazon.com/dp/B005G32JRI
2. Sensitive Stories of Corporate World (Management Case Studies) https://www.amazon.com/dp/B004KABBMM
3. Sensitive Stories of Corporate World (Volume 2) (Management Case Studies) https://www.amazon.com/dp/B072PT1JGP
4. Sensitive Stories of Corporate World (Volumes 1 & 2 Combined) (Management Case Studies) https://www.amazon.com/dp/B07G5G4WRP
5. Classic Management Games, Exercises, Energizers and Icebreakers https://www.amazon.com/dp/B004OEKF0I
6. Classic Management Games, Exercises, Energizers and Icebreakers (Volume 2) https://www.amazon.com/dp/B007CJESMY
7. Classic Team Building Games, Exercises, Energizers and Icebreakers https://www.amazon.com/dp/B00MJC8SPQ
8. 101 Classic Management Games, Exercises, Energizers and Icebreakers https://www.amazon.com/dp/B07HFZ19V4
9. Stress? No Way!! (Handbook on Stress Management) https://www.amazon.com/dp/B005LV37JO
10. HSoftware (Shyam Bhatawdekar's Effectiveness Model) https://www.amazon.com/dp/B0051OS2TQ
11. Competency Management (Competency Matrix and Competencies) https://www.amazon.com/dp/B00VNTZKK2
12. Soft Skills You Can't Do Without (Goal Setting, Time Management, Assertiveness and Anger Management) https://www.amazon.com/dp/B00KE5WUXQ

13. Team Building and Teamwork
https://www.amazon.com/dp/B09LRZS4QM

14. Essentials of Work Study (Method Study and Work Measurement) https://www.amazon.com/dp/B008RYYWJQ

15. Essentials of Time Management (Taking Control of Your Life) https://www.amazon.com/dp/B009WXI1ZW

16. Essentials of 5S Housekeeping
https://www.amazon.com/dp/B00A6HCVRM

17. Essentials of Quality Circles
https://www.amazon.com/dp/B00ACHOHGE

18. Essentials of Goal Setting
https://www.amazon.com/dp/B00AP1DEX0

19. Essentials of Anger Management
https://www.amazon.com/dp/B00AZFLIII

20. Essentials of Assertive Behavior
https://www.amazon.com/dp/B00C5UMCEU

21. Essentials of Performance Management and Performance Appraisal https://www.amazon.com/dp/B00DA06UTM

22. Health Essentials (Health Is Wealth)
https://www.amazon.com/dp/B00E5IFCSS

23. Essentials of Effective Communication
https://www.amazon.com/dp/B071XJ823H

24. The Romance of Intimacy (How to Enhance Intimacy in a Relationship?)
https://www.amazon.com/dp/B007NGBBOI

25. **How to Succeed in Job Interviews and Promotions (Question Bank Included)**
https://www.amazon.com/dp/B0DP31ZXWQ

Novels, Stories, Poems and Biographies

26. Funny (and Not So Funny) Short Stories
https://www.amazon.com/dp/B004MDLTPQ

27. Stories Children Will Love (Volume 1: Bhanu-Shanu-Kaju-Biju and Dholu Ram Gadbad Singh)
https://www.amazon.com/dp/B0071J74CA

28. My Father (Biography)
https://www.amazon.com/dp/B019A4L8KM

29. Love Knows No Bounds
https://www.amazon.com/dp/B00HO2KFMA

30. The Peace Crusaders
https://www.amazon.com/dp/B00Q3OBIY4

31. The New World Order (Emergence of a Star)
https://www.amazon.com/dp/B085MYGH63

32. Dawn of a New Era https://www.amazon.com/dp/B09CNLNFGC

33. Bouquet of My Favorite Stories (Six Short Novels)
https://www.amazon.com/dp/B0B1VNSG1Q

34. सीमाओं के परे: एक अलग प्रेम कहानी
https://www.amazon.com/dp/B07D6BQXYW

35. अमन के सिपाही https://www.amazon.com/dp/B07RC4CV2R

36. नई सुबह, नई रोशनी https://www.amazon.com/dp/B09CMXHJ6W

37. मेरी पसंद की कहानियों का गुलदस्ता (छह लघु उपन्यास)
https://www.amazon.com/dp/B0B1VM3MN8

38. अभिजात प्रेम: एक वेगळी प्रेम कथा
https://www.amazon.com/dp/B089FKP6GC

39. दुरितांचे तिमिर जावो https://www.amazon.com/dp/B091N8S1JX

40. होत उष:काल हा https://www.amazon.com/dp/B09CMWP7VR

41. गुलदस्ता आवडत्या कथांचा (सहा लघु कादंबऱ्या)
https://www.amazon.com/dp/B0B1VH4B1H

42. Women Power https://www.amazon.com/dp/B0BY927N5D

43. नारी शक्ति https://www.amazon.com/dp/B0BYFF4WMC

44. स्त्री शक्ती https://www.amazon.com/dp/B0BYKG9WB1

45. आपकी हमारी छोटी बड़ी कविताएँ
https://www.amazon.com/dp/B0D7TQBCR3

Travelogues

46. Travelogue: Scandinavia, Russia
https://www.amazon.com/dp/B008QYMS3E

47. Travelogue: Europe https://www.amazon.com/dp/B01ID2255Y

48. यूरोप की सैर https://www.amazon.com/dp/B0CLRZB8HW

49. Travelogue: Central Europe
https://www.amazon.com/dp/B07YVFND27

50. Travelogue: Egypt (Mysteries of Egypt)
https://www.amazon.com/dp/B08NZKR7DL

To Our Family

Shyam Bhatawdekar   Dr Kalpana Bhatawdekar

Work Study comprising of its two main branches Method Study and Work Measurement remains, even to date, the most fundamental system of introducing continual improvements in effectiveness, efficiency and overall productivity. It is the forerunner of the latter-day systems and techniques like Kaizen, TQM and Business Process Reengineering etc.

Therefore, a thorough knowledge of Work Study becomes imperative. To facilitate gaining the knowledge in this important subject in the shortest possible time, the authors Shyam Bhatawdekar and Dr Kalpana Bhatawdekar included only the "essentials" of Work Study in the book.

The authors are top-notch business executives, highly sought after business and management consultants, eminent management gurus, authentic human behavior experts and prolific authors. And so the book "Essentials of Work Study" becomes an authentic document on the subject.

To read more by the authors, refer their websites: https://proficient.io and http://management-universe.blogspot.com

Essentials of Work Study
(Method Study and Work Measurement)

Shyam Bhatawdekar
Dr Kalpana Bhatawdekar

Published by Publishing Division of

Prodcons Group

8, Pranjal Society, Shiv Tirth Nagar, Paud Road, Pune 411038 (India)

Email: prodcons@prodcons.com

For other web publications, refer: http://management-universe.blogspot.com and https://proficient.io

Copyright © with the authors Shyam Bhatawdekar and Dr Kalpana Bhatawdekar

All rights reserved

No reproduction without permission in whole or in part in any form

Contents

1. Organization's Most Important Jobs
2. Value for Money to Customers (VFM)
3. Productivity
4. Work Study: The Pioneering Technique of Improving Value for Money and Productivity
5. Method Study
6. Objectives of Method Study
7. Different Recording Techniques
8. Seven Steps of Carrying Out Method Study
9. Some Details on the Step 3 of the Process of Method Study i.e. Examine
10. Some Details on the Step 5 of the Process of Method Study i.e. Define New (Improved) Method
11. Some Details on the Step 6 of the Process of Method Study i.e. Install New (Improved) Method
12. Classic Example: Early Application of Method Study by Taylor
13. Motion Economy Principles
14. Classic Example: Early Application of Motion and Time Study by Gilbreth
15. Work Measurement
16. Fair Day's Work
17. Objectives of Work Measurement
18. Some Techniques of Work Measurement
19. Conceptual Framework for Carrying Out Work Measurement
20. Steps in Carrying Out Work Measurement (Determining the Standard Time)
21. Work Simplification: Vital Aspect of Work Study

Essentials of Work Study (Method Study and Work Measurement)

Organization's Most Important Jobs

Two most important jobs that every organization should do for its existence and growth are given below. All other jobs done in an organization should be directed towards these two:

- Finding the customers and retaining them (an organization can survive only if it has customers). For this, continually providing maximum value for money (VFM) to the customers to sustain highest level of customer satisfaction.
- Improving overall productivity and thereby, minimizing the overall costs as much below the price as possible and thus maximizing profits (surplus). What is the big fun if you cannot create reasonable profits or surplus?

Now it will be a good idea to understand the two important terms used in the foregoing paragraphs i.e. "value for money (VFM)" and "productivity".

Value for Money to Customers (VFM)

Essentially five factors provide value to the customer for his money. These are: quality of goods and services sold, service level provided to the customer, relationship with the customer, price of goods and services and lead time (the elapsed time between the placing of order by a customer to the receipt of the ordered goods and services by him from the supplier).

Better quality of goods and services, higher service level, closer relationship with customer, lower price and lower delivery time improve the value for money to customer. More the value for money to the customer more is the customer satisfaction. Higher customer satisfaction in turn means repeat orders from the same customer and attracting more customers due to word of mouth publicity.

Therefore the equation for value for money to customer will be as given below:

Value to customer (VFM) = (Total quality "Q" X Total service inclusive of pre, during and post customer service "S" X Relationship with customers "R") divided by (Price "P" X Lead time "L")

i.e. ***VFM*** = (Q X S X R) / (P X L)

Therefore, value for money to customers should be continually enhanced by continual improvements in:

- Quality (Q)
- Price (P): Price being normally an outcome of the market forces of supply and demand cannot be ordinarily increased. Therefore in order to make better profits the overall costs should be kept well below those price levels. And if costs can be further controlled, prices can also be reduced to gain price advantage over the competitors and yet achieving the desired profits.
- Delivery (L)
- Service (S)
- Relations (R)

Key point is "continual improvement" of these five factors.

Productivity

Productivity is measure of output per unit of input.

Therefore, the equation for **Productivity (P)** = Output quantity (O) divided by Input quantity (I)

i.e. $P = O / I$

It is important that the output should be an acceptable output to the users or customers. So enters the quality. Therefore, in order to reckon and emphasize qualitative changes in output and input, the equation of productivity will read as given below:

Productivity = Output quality and quantity / Input quality and quantity

Productivity, thus, can be improved by three ways:

- Increase output and keep input constant.
- Keep output constant and decrease input.
- Increase both, output as well as input making sure that the proportion of increase in output is more than that of input.

Normally, outputs are: goods (products) and/or services.

Normally, inputs are various resources: man (labor and management), machine (equipment), material, money (all types of capital) and also, time and information.

Work Study: The Pioneering Technique of Improving Value for Money and Productivity

Work Study, under the major discipline of industrial engineering, emerged as the earliest effectiveness and efficiency technique that even to date remains the basic to all other techniques that developed later. Kaizen, Total Quality Management (TQM) and Business Process Engineering (BPR) etc basically use the underlying principles of Work Study. Work Study was the sequel to Taylor's famous scientific management.

Work Study is defined as the systematic examination of the methods of carrying on activities so as to improve the effective use of resources and to set up standards of performance for the activities being carried out.

Work Study has two major branches:

1. Method Study
2. Work Measurement

Method Study

Method Study is the systematic recording and critical examination of existing and proposed ways of doing work, as a means of developing and applying easier and more effective methods and reducing overall costs.

It uses different sets of techniques and tools to do so.

Objectives of Method Study

Given below are some of the major objectives to be achieved by application of Method Study:

- Improvement in use of all the inputs i.e. men, machines, materials, money and also, time and information.
- Economy in human effort and reduction of unnecessary fatigue.
- Layout improvements.
- Improvement in design of plant and equipment.

- Improvement in safety standards and procedures.
- Development of better working environment.

Seven Steps of Carrying Out Method Study: The Process

It is easy to carry out Method Study if you do it systematically. Following seven steps are prescribed for carrying out Method Study in the order given below. For the best results, the suggested order in which these steps should be executed, must be strictly maintained:

1. *Define* existing method.
2. *Record* existing method.
3. *Examine* existing method.
4. *Develop* new method.
5. *Define* new method.
6. *Install* new method.
7. *Maintain* new method.

You can easily remember these seven steps in the order mentioned above if you can remember the acronym "*DREDDIM*" for these steps.

Different Recording Techniques

Names of some the important recording techniques are as follows:

- Outline process charts
- Flow process chart: man type, material type, equipment type
- Two handed process chart
- Multiple activity chart: using time scale
- Simo chart: using time scale
- Flow diagrams
- String diagrams
- Cyclegraph
- Chronocyclegraph
- Travel Chart

Some Details on Step 3 of the Process of Method Study i.e. Examine

'Examine' step uses questioning technique. Each activity of the method under examination is subjected to systematic and progressive series of questions. There are two types of questions asked:

1. Primary questions
2. Secondary questions

Primary Questions

Questions are asked and answers found out on:

- *Purpose* for which activity is being done.
- *Place* at which activity is being carried out.
- *Sequence* in which activity is being performed.
- *Person* by whom activity is being rendered.
- *Means* by which activity is being accomplished.

This primary examination is carried out with a view to

- Eliminate,
- Combine,
- Rearrange and/or
- Simplify the activities.

Secondary Questions

During the secondary questions, answers to the primary questions are subjected to further query to determine whether possible alternatives of purpose, place, sequence, persons and means are practicable and preferred as a means of improvement upon the existing method.

1. Purpose:

- What is done?
- Why is it done?
- What else might be done?
- What should be done?

2. Place:

- Where is it done?
- Why is it done there?
- Where else might it be done?
- Where should it be done?

3. Sequence:

- When is it done?
- Why is it done?
- When might it be done?
- When should it be done?

4. Person:

- Who does it?
- Why does that person do it?
- Who else might do it?
- Who should do it?

5. Means:

- How is it done?
- Why is it done that way?
- How else might it be done?
- How should it be done?

Some Details on Step 5 of the Process of Method Study i.e. Define New (Improved) Method

A report on new improved method should be prepared. It should include:

- Descriptions of the new method and the existing method.

- Relative costs in material, labor and overheads of the new method and the existing method and expected savings.
- Cost of installing the new method, including cost of new equipment and of re-laying out shops or working areas.
- Diagram of the work place layout.
- Tools and equipment to be used and diagrams of jigs/fixtures etc.
- Executive actions required to implement the new method.

Some Details on Step 6 of the Process of Method Study i.e. Install New (Improved) Method

This step involves the "buying in" of the new method by the concerned persons of an organization. It also emphasizes on review and control action on implementation of the change.

- Gaining acceptance of the change by the Management.
- Gaining acceptance of the change by the workers.

- Keeping a close eye on the progress of implementation of the new method till it starts running satisfactorily.

Classic Example: Early Application of Method Study by Taylor

Tons handled on piecework during the year ended 30th April 1901: 924,040

- Cost of handling these materials: $30,798
- Former cost per year: $67,215
- Net saving: $36,417
- Average cost per ton: now $0.033, formerly $0.072
- Average earnings per man per day: now $1.88, formerly $1.15
- Average tons handled per man per day: now 57, formerly 16
- Number of men: now 140, formerly 400 to 600

Motion Economy Principles

As an important part of Method Study, Frank Gilbreth and his wife Lillian Gilbreth, through their various experiments, institutionalized **Motion and Time Study** through their famous motion economy principles. (You may find it interesting to refer their biographical 1950 film "Cheaper by the Dozen" and also the book by the same title).

If one can study the motions and micro motions performed in carrying out an activity and economize on them i.e. try to reduce them, then the time taken for the activity can be significantly reduced.

For this, the movements are classified in 5 classes as given below:

- Class 1: Body members moved in this class are fingers and the pivot is knuckle.
- Class 2: Body members moved in this class are hands and fingers and the pivot is wrist.
- Class 3: Body members moved in this class are forearms, hands and fingers and the pivot is elbow.
- Class 4: Body members moved in this class are upper arms, forearms, hands and fingers and the pivot is shoulder.

- Class 5: Body members moved in this class are torso, upper arms, forearms, hands and fingers and the pivot is trunk.

Further, Gilbreth came out with the idea of conducting micro motion study. To facilitate it, a set of fundamental motions required for a worker to perform a manual operation was defined. The set consists of 18 elements, each describing a standardized activity. The set is called "therblig" (read Gilbreth in reverse order and you get this term "therblig" with "th" treated as one letter). These are: listed below:

- Search
- Find
- Select
- Grasp
- Hold
- Position
- Assemble
- Use
- Disassemble
- Inspect
- Transport loaded
- Transport unloaded

- Pre-position for next operation
- Release load
- Unavoidable delay
- Avoidable delay
- Plan
- Rest to overcome fatigue

Classic Example: Early Application of Motion and Time Study by Gilbreth

Frank Gilbreth designed a special scaffold and a new brick laying procedure that reduced the movements needed from 18 to 5 and in one case to 2.

The worker's productivity increased from laying 120 bricks per hour to laying 350 bricks per hour. The new procedure also decreased fatigue.

Work Measurement

Work Measurement is the application of techniques designed to establish the time for a qualified worker to carry out a task at a defined rate of working or at a defined level of performance.

It measures the time taken in performance of an operation or a series of operations and it can separate out ineffective time from effective time.

Thus ineffective time can be studied and by way of Method Study described in earlier paragraphs, the ineffective operations can be reduced or eliminated.

Fair Day's Work

Fair day's work is defined as the amount of work that can be produced by a qualified worker/employee when working at normal pace and effectively utilizing his time and where work is not restricted by process limitations.

In order to effect improvements in productivity and value for money to the customer, an organization and a worker are legitimate in expecting a fair day's work.

Objectives of Work Measurement

Given below are some of the major objectives to be achieved by application of Work Measurement:

- Finding ineffective time in an activity or a process (series of activities).
- Setting standard (norms) for output level.
- Evaluating workers' performance.
- Assessing and planning manpower needs.
- Determining available capacity.
- Comparing various work methods.
- Facilitating operations scheduling.
- Establishing wage incentive schemes.

Some Techniques of Work Measurement

The main techniques that are often used to carry out Work Measurement are:

- Stopwatch time study
- Work sampling
- Predetermined time standards (PTS)
- Standard Data

Conceptual Framework for Carrying Out Work Measurement

It is essential to understand the following concepts in order to undertake work measurement exercise in any organization:

- **Qualified worker:** Qualified worker is one who is accepted as having the necessary physical attributes, who possess the required intelligence and education and who has acquired the necessary skills and knowledge to carry out the work in hand to satisfactory standards of safety, quantity and quality.
- **Standard rating:** Rating is the assessment of the worker's rate of working relative to the observer's concept of the rate corresponding to standard pace (or standard rate).
- **Standard performance (pace or rate):** It is the rate of output which a qualified worker will naturally achieve without over-exertion as an average over the working day or shift, provided that he knows and adheres to the specified method and provided that he is motivated to apply himself to his work. The time

taken to achieve the standard performance by the qualified worker is called "standard time".

Steps in Carrying Out Work Measurement (Determining the Standard Time): The Process

It is easy to carry out Work Measurement if you do it systematically. Following eight steps are prescribed in carrying out Work Measurement in the order given below. It is important to strictly follow the order in which these eight steps should be executed:

1. Obtain and record all available information about the job, the worker and the surrounding conditions likely to affect the execution of the work.
2. Record the complete description of the method and break it down into elements.
3. Measure with a stopwatch and record the time taken by the worker to perform each element of the operation.
4. Assess the rating of the worker.
5. Extend the observed time to "basic time" by factorizing the actual time (observed time) by the assessed rating.

6. Determine the allowances (e.g. personal allowances, relaxation/fatigue allowances, allowances for the working conditions etc) to be made over and above the "basic time" for the operation. International Labor Organization (ILO) has suggested these allowances and their quantification. The companies implementing Work Measurement should be guided by these standards.
7. Apply those allowances on the "basic time".
8. Thus, determine the "standard time" for the operation.

Work Simplification: Vital Aspect of Work Study

Work simplification is a systematic approach to improve effectiveness and efficiency by focusing on the following steps of the process (Also refer pages 18-21 for the primary and secondary questions that need to be asked and their answers to be found while carrying out work simplification):

1. **Identify and Clarify the Problem**: First, understand the current method/process and identify areas where waste or ineffectiveness/inefficiencies exist. For this, you may like to create a business

process map or flowchart to study and understand the flow of work.

2. **Eliminate**: Next step is to identify and remove any non-value adding and unnecessary activities. This will involve simplifying processes, eliminating redundant activities and/or streamlining documentation.

3. **Combine**: If an activity cannot be eliminated, explore ways and means to combine it with another activity. This step will involve merging certain activities/tasks, consolidating them or using automation to reduce manual workload.

4. **Rearrange**: Now consider changing the sequence of steps and activities/operations to improve the workflow. This will involve reorganizing, rearranging and/or shuffling steps/operations to reduce backtracking, improve ergonomics and optimize the use of machines/equipment.

5. **Simplify**: After performing the abovementioned steps of eliminating, combining and rearranging, now make the remaining tasks/operations as easy and efficient/effective as possible. This could involve using tools, jigs, fixtures, templates and automation to simplify tasks/activities.

6. **Evaluate and Implement**: After making changes using the steps 1 through 5 mentioned earlier, measure and evaluate the results to ensure that the improvements you introduced have been effective as per the plans and to the intended degree. Implement the improvements and make sure that they are maintainable and sustainable.
7. **Standardize**: Once the process has been simplified, it is necessary to standardize it to ensure that the simplified process is used the way it has been standardized and possibility of creeping in of inefficiencies in future is prevented.
8. **Continuous Improvement**: Work simplification as described here is not a one-time job. In fact it is an ongoing process of planning, designing and implementing continuous improvement. It is also important to review and update the implemented process periodically to stay up-to-date as per changing conditions and requirements.

www.ingramcontent.com/pod-product-compliance
Lightning Source LLC
Chambersburg PA
CBHW061522180526
45171CB00001B/287